SNACKS

A Comedy

by
LEONARD GERSHE

SAMUEL FRENCH, INC.
45 West 25th Street   NEW YORK 10010
7623 Sunset Boulevard HOLLYWOOD 90046
LONDON   TORONTO

Copyright ©, 1985, by Leonard Gershe

ALL RIGHTS RESERVED

ACT ONE

Scene One

A Saturday morning in May

Scene Two

Later that day

ACT TWO

The next morning

CHARACTERS

MARCO FABRIZIO

BETTY NEAL

HENRY RITTER

VINNIE FABRIZIO

SNACKS
ACT ONE
Scene One

A small, neighborhood coffee shop in lower east side Manhattan. Right, the street window with the word SNACKS in chipped gold lettering, backwards. On the wall below the window there is a pay phone on the wall. This wall and the left wall must be angled for full visibility. Up, left of the window is the front door, glass paned with a roller shade. Upstage is the counter with several stools in front of it. Under the counter, out of view, are shelves, a sink and an ice cream freezer, the top of which is visible when opened. Behind the counter is a work area with a large coffee urn, a gas burner and grill and work space. Right of this there is an old refrigerator. Left of the work space there is a door leading to a storage room. Left of this is another door marked REST ROOM. There is a small formica-topped table and two chairs against the right wall and a similar arrangement against the left wall.

AT RISE: A morning in late spring. The table and chairs for the left wall have been moved away from the wall, chairs stacked on the table, to make room for a painter's drop cloth. Close to the wall, which has been partially painted, there is a wood folding ladder with a fold out work shelf on which there is a can of white paint and a paint brush. A sign hangs on the front door reading OPEN, so it reads CLOSED outside.

There is no one on stage. A moment later, BETTY NEAL, a pretty young woman, walks past the street window carrying a shopping bag. She stops at the door, studies the sign for a moment, then tries the door. It opens and she enters the shop. She looks around for a moment, taking it all in.

BETTY. Hello? *(She sets her shopping bag on the counter stool nearest the door. She looks at the OPEN sign on the door, crosses to the door and turns the sign around so that it reads CLOSED inside. She crosses to the storage room. opens the door.)* Anyone here?

(She closes the door and starts to open the rest room door when she hears the toilet flushing. She crosses, quickly, to the stool next to her shopping bag and sits. A moment later, MARCO FABRIZIO emerges from the rest room. He is an attractive young man, dressed in paint-stained jeans. He doesn't notice BETTY as he starts toward the ladder.)

BETTY. Good morning.
MARCO. *(turns, startled)* Who are you?!
BETTY. Betty Neal. *(smiling)* How do you do?
MARCO. What're you doin' here? How'd you get in?
BETTY. The door wasn't locked.
MARCO. *(glancing at the door)* It shoulda been. I'm sorry but we're closed. You shoulda looked at the sign in the door before you walked in. *(pointing to the sign)* See — it says closed. *(He looks at the sign and does a take. BETTY smiles, quietly. MARCO crosses to the door and turns the sign around.)* We're closed 'til Tuesday. *(crossing toward the ladder)* Ya can see I'm paintin' the place. Come back Tuesday, ya can

have anything ya want.

BETTY. I didn't come in to eat. I came in to ask a favor. I need help.

MARCO. Come back Tuesday.

BETTY. Tuesday will be too late.

MARCO. What is it?

BETTY. My refrigerator died some time during the night and I can't get anyone to fix it before Monday. *(She picks up the shopping bag.)* I have a small fortune in frozen food here. It will defrost and go bad.

MARCO. Sure — but what d'ya want me to do?

BETTY. Have you got a freezer?

MARCO. Only an ice cream freezer.

BETTY. Well, that should be all right. Please let me leave these things in your freezer. It'll just be for a few days.

MARCO. I don't know if I'm allowed to do that.

BETTY. I see. Perhaps if I spoke to the manager... What's his name?

MARCO. Marco Fabrizio.

BETTY. Is he around?

MARCO. Yeah, I'm here. I'm *Marco.*

BETTY. Oh. Well ... what if I spoke to the owner?

MARCO. I'm the owner. This place is owned by me and my brother, Vinnie.

BETTY. Well, if you're the manager and the owner, then what's the problem? I'll be happy to pay you, if that's what you mean.

MARCO. It ain't a question of money. It is a question of that this is a business which caters to the public, so we got all kinds o' inspectors comin' in from time to time. Building inspectors and health inspectors. I'm not sure that it's legal for me to have someone else's food on the premises. Maybe ya need a license for that. Ya need a license for everything else. I mean it could be against the law. *(BETTY looks at him for a moment, then moves close to him.)*

BETTY. *(insidously)* Oh, come on— have you no sense of *adventure?* Have you no *derring-do?!* Haven't you ever wanted to do something everyone says *don't* do? Don't cross against the light. Don't walk on the grass. Don't put someone else's food in your freezer. This could be your year of living dangerously!

MARCO. Listen! I like adventure just as much as the next guy an' Steven Spielberg gives me all I need ... an' what the hell is derring-do?

BETTY. Bravery ... *courage.* You have it or you have it not. Spielberg can't give it to you. *(She has an idea.)* I know what! My father is a judge, why don't you ...

MARCO. *(interrupting)* Your father is a judge?

BETTY. Yes.

MARCO. You got a father who's a judge an' you go around breakin' the law. Nice.

BETTY. I don't break laws. I just bend a few rules. *(gesturing toward the phone)* Call him and ask him what the rap is for having somone else's food on your premises. Maybe it's just a fine, in which case I will pay it. The number is area code two one five ... three eight three ...

MARCO. *(interrupting)* Where is area code two one five?

BETTY. Philadelphia. Call him and explain the situation. Hurry before he heads for the golf club.

MARCO. Lady, I'm not callin' your father. You call him.

BETTY. I would, but I'm not speaking to my family at the moment.

MARCO. Well, neither am I, so let's forget it. I'm sorry. I wish I could help ya. Ya seem like a nice person.

BETTY. There's no changing your mind?

MARCO. Sorry.

BETTY. *(thinks for a moment)* Have I exhausted every avenue?

MARCO. I don't know. Go try Avenue B. *(BETTY picks up her shopping bag, forlornly.)*

BETTY. Obviously, this isn't my day. I'm sorry to have bothered you. *(She crosses to MARCO, holding out her hand.)* Nice to have met you, Marco. *(BETTY stands, holding her hand out. MARCO looks at her and takes pity on her. He throws up his hands.)*

MARCO. Okay, I'll do it!

BETTY. *(excitedly)* You'll call my father? Really?

MARCO. No! I'll put your food in the freezer.

BETTY. Oh God! *(She punches his arm affectionately)* You have got derring-do!! Alexander the Great had it ... Lindenbergh had it ...

MARCO. Yeah, but lemme tell ya something—don't make a habit o' this

BETTY. You have my word. *(She shoves the shopping bag into his arms.)* You are really angelic, Marco. Thank you, thank you. *(She kisses him on the cheek, hurries toward the door.)*

MARCO. Hey, wait a minute!! *(BETTY freezes.)*

BETTY. *(turning)* What?

MARCO. Why don't ya kiss your food goodbye, too?!

BETTY. What do you mean?

MARCO. Don't ya want a receipt for criisake?

BETTY. No. I don't need a receipt.

MARCO. *(nodding toward a stool)* Just sit down there, please. *(BETTY crosses to the stool and sits as MARCO carries the shopping bag behind the counter.)* Look, I'm doin' you a favor, wouldn't ya say?

BETTY. Yes, but ...

MARCO. Then we're gonna do this the right way. I don't know you. You don't know me. Business is business ... or would ya like to forget the whole deal?

BETTY. No, no, do it your way ... but don't let it take too long. I should show up at work sometime today.

MARCO. It won't take long. I'm just gonna itemize the stuff. *(He finds a pad and pencil on the counter behind him, then reaches in to the bag and brings out two packages.)* Macaroni an' cheese. Two packages. Net weight twelve ounces each.

BETTY. You don't have to list the weight, do you?

MARCO. *(writing on the pad)* No. We can skip the weight. *(He opens the lid of the freezer and drops the packages in. He takes two more packages from the bag.)* Creamed chipped beef. Two packages.

BETTY. I think there are three.

MARCO. *(after rummaging through)* No. Only two creamed chipped beefs.

BETTY. That's right. I ate one Wednesday night.

MARCO. Ya see! That's why this is important. You would've accused me o' takin' one creamed chipped beef.

BETTY. *(impatiently)* Yes, yes. *(aloud to herself)* God, I wish I smoked.

MARCO. *(writing on the pad)* Okay, two creamed chipped beefs ... not three. *(He drops them in to the freezer and takes another package from the bag.)* Green pepper steak with rice, Chinese style. *(shaking his head)* Jesus!

BETTY. It happens to be very good.

MARCO. I bet. *(He notes this on the pad and drops it in the freezer. He takes out another package.)* Chicken chow mein ... boil in bag. Boil in bag??!!

BETTY. It comes sealed in a plastic bag and you heat it by putting the bag in boiling water. It's very convenient.

MARCO. Food should be good, not convenient. *(He notes the chow mein on the pad.)*

BETTY. Please—just itemize, never mind the editorials.

MARCO. *(taking out the next package)* Another chow mein, boil in bag. Okay, that makes two o' those. *(He makes the correction on the pad.)*

BETTY. I haven't had any breakfast. Do you think I might have a cup of coffee?

MARCO. Why not? *(He turns to the work counter behind him and presses the lever on an electric kettle. He reaches under the counter and brings up two mugs?)* Instant okay?

BETTY. It's the only kind I drink.

MARCO. Sure—it's convenient. *(Betty opens her shoulder bag, takes out a change purse and opens it.)*

MARCO. What're ya doin'?

BETTY. Getting money to pay you. How much is it?

MARCO. C'mom, will ya?!

BETTY. I insist. Business is business.

MARCO. I'm not open for business. After Tuesday, you can pay. *(He takes another package from the shopping bag.)* Chicken paprikash with noodles. *(noting it on the pad)*

What's that—Polish?

BETTY. Hungarian. *(MARCO drops the package into the freezer as the kettle whistles. He turns it off, opens a jar of instant coffee and fixes coffee in the two mugs. He places BETTY'S mug in front of her.)*

BETTY. Thank you. *(She sips her coffee.)*

MARCO. I'd like to ask you somethin'—can't you cook?

BETTY. No.

MARCO. Nothing at all?

BETTY. Nothing whatsoever. Do you cook?

MARCO. Like a nightingale!

BETTY. That good?

MARCO. I learned from my mother. Didn't ya ever watch your mother cook?

BETTY. My mother can't cook.

MARCO. *(amazed)* I never heard of a mother what can't cook. So, who cooked—your father?

BETTY. Dad can't boil water.

MARCO. So, when you were growing up, what did ya do—eat out every night?

BETTY. We always had a cook.

MARCO. You always had a cook? Your own private cook—just for your family?

BETTY. Lots of people have cooks.

MARCO. No, I don't think *lots*. Ya know, I always thought there was somethin' classy about you.

BETTY. What do you mean "always"?

MARCO. I've seen ya before. You been livin' in this neighborhood—what? Four, five months?

BETTY. Almost six.

MARCO. I've seen you walk by here.

BETTY. I pass be here every day.

MARCO. *(pointedly)* Yeah—but ya never come in.

BETTY. Well—I'm certainly in now. Can we finish the inventory?

MARCO. Sure. *(He takes two packages from the shopping bag.)* How come ya don't have any Italian food?

BETTY. You're coming to it.

MARCO. *(looking at package)* Oh, yeah ... here we go. Chicken cacciatore with spaghetti. *(noting this on pad)* You oughta taste mine. Mine is even better than my mom's, God rest her soul. My brother, Vinnie—he's a fussy eater—he freaks out over my cooking.

BETTY. I'm not fussy. I'll eat anything I can defrost.

MARCO. Anyone ever tell yaya eat like an Eskimo? *(He takes another package from the shopping bag.)* Lasagne with meat sauce ... boil in bag. *(taking out two more packages)* Ya got three o' that crap.

BETTY. Ah! I knew I had three of something.

MARCO. *(He notes these on the pad, drops them in the freeer and takes four frozen juice cartons from the bag.)* And four frozen orange juice. That's it. *(He notes these on the pad and drops them in the freezer.)* Finished. *(He pushes the pad and pencil toward BETTY.)* Ya wanna look that over an' please sign your name.

BETTY. I'm sure it's all right.

MARCO. Then sign you name, if ya don't mind. *(BETTY signs.)* An' put down your address an' telephone number.

BETTY. Why do you need my telephone number?

MARCO. In case of emergency.

BETTY. What sort of emergency?

MARCO. Somebody could break in here an' take your food. A person could reach in to the freezer while my back is turned. We could have a fire ... a flood. There could be a power outage an' maybe ...

BETTY. All right, all right. And world war three could break out. *(She writes on the pad as MARCO freshens her mug of coffee.)*

MARCO. Don't worry. I ain't in to obscene phone calls. I got anything obscene to say, I'll say it right to your face.

BETTY. I don't doubt that. *(She pushes the pad and pencil back to MARCO.)* Does it have to be witnessed or notarized?

MARCO. *(without looking at the pad)* No, that's fine. *(He looks BETTY over, appraisingly as she gets off the stool.)*

BETTY. I really do appreciate what you're doing. I'll be back just as soon as I get the fridge fixed.

MARCO. Hey, drink your coffee. Ya can't face that jungle out there on just one cup o' coffee. *(He crosses right to the table and chairs.)* C'mon over here. You'll be more comfortable.

BETTY. I have to be at work at eleven.

MARCO. *(taking the chairs off the table and setting them in place)* Ya got plenty o' time. *(He holds a chair out for her. BETTY picks up her coffee and crosses to the table.)*

BETTY. What about your painting?

MARCO. I can paint while we talk. I'll be finished in plenty o' time to open Tuesday. *(BETTY sits at the table.)* I just gotta finish that wall and do the trim. No sweat. *(MARCO crosses to the ladder and resumes painting the wall.)*

So—uh—whatdya do with yourself? Ya mentioned work.

BETTY. I work at the Met.

MARCO. Oh, yeah? You an opera singer?

BETTY. No, the Metropolitan museum.

MARCO. The Metropolitan museum of art? That one?

BETTY. Yes, that one.

MARCO. Would ya believe I been in New York all my life an' I never been there?

BETTY. Yes, I believe it. If you ever decide to come, you can find me in the book shop. I sell books, posters, things like that. It's a part time job. Actually, I'm at Columbia.

MARCO. Columbia broadcasting? CBS?

BETTY. Columbia University. I'm taking my masters in higher education.

MARCO. *(impressed)* Higher education, huh? I never been there either. I dropped outta school when I was fifteen.

BETTY. What did you do?

MARCO. Just hung around. Sometimes I came in here an' helped my pop out. He useta own this place before he died. How's your coffee? *(He climbs down the ladder.)*

BETTY. Delicious.

MARCO. *(crossing to behind the counter)* Ready for more?

BETTY. Not yet.

MARCO. *(He picks up his coffee and sips.)* I wish now that I'da finished school. The time was just wasted. Ya know what I mean? *(He glances at the pad, picks it up and reads, frowning.)* Hey—I thought ya said your name was Betty.

BETTY. It is.

MARCO. Ya wrote here Elizbeth Neal.

BETTY. Betty is a nickname for Elizabeth. When I sign important documents like that, I use my full legal name.

MARCO. So, what do ya like to ya called?

BETTY. *(finishes her coffee, rises and carries the mug to the counter)* I don't really care. Elizabeth has so many diminutives and I've been called all of them—Betty, Liz, Lizzie, Beth, Bess, Bessie. *(She hands her mug to MARCO and he refills it.)* The only one I really don't like is Beth. Beth sounds like someone pale and fragile and helpless. It's just too "Little Women" to suit me.

MARCO. What little women?

BETTY. You know—"Little Women." Beth, Amy, Meg and Jo. *(MARCO places the mug in front of her and looks at her, blankly.)* I can't believe you don't know "Little Women."

MARCO. Look, a lotta people come in here. I don't get all the names.

BETTY. I'm talking about a book by Louisa May Alcott.

MARCO. *(returning to the ladder and the painting)* Wasn't it a movie?

BETTY. About a hundred times. Marco, do you read?

MARCO. Sure I can read.

BETTY. Ah, you *can,* but *do* you?

MARCO. Yes, I do. I like to read magazines an' newspapers. I like the sports pages an' I like the columns like Suzy an' Liz Smith. I like to know what the beautiful people are doin'.

BETTY. Why?

MARCO. 'Cause what they're doin' is more interestin' than what I'm doin'.

BETTY. Sports pages and columns are amusing, but don't you ever want to read something more nourishing.

MARCO. I read like you eat—boil in bag. *(BETTY crosses to the counter, sets her coffee mug down and sits on a stool, facing MARCO.)*

BETTY. If I'd never read a book, I wouldn't make jokes about it. Ignorance may be bliss, but it isn't funny. *(MARCO looks at her, sharply, climbs down the ladder and crosses to her.)*

MARCO. Lemme tell ya somethin'—I ain't stupid.

BETTY. I never said you were stupid ... and I don't think you are.

MARCO. Vinnie says there are two kinds o' smart. There's book smart—like you an' there's street smart—like me.

BETTY. Can't you be both?

MARCO. Are you both?

BETTY. I'm working on street smart.

MARCO. Yeah—I noticed.

BETTY. What do you mean?

MARCO. (pointing to the sign in the door) I mean like turning that sign around to try to make me think *I* did it.

BETTY. *(grinning)* Damn! I thought I got away with that.

MARCO. What ya *shoulda* done was to walk in here with

your frozen food an' when ya didn't see anyone around, go over to the freezer and dump the stuff in then got your ass outta here before I came outta the john ... an' I wouldn't've known anything about it 'til Tuesday! *That's street smart!!*

BETTY. To hell with higher education ... I can learn more from you.

MARCO. Ya better—'specially in this neighborhood. *(He looks at her, oddly.)* What are you doin' here, anyway? Where do ya live?

BETTY. I wrote my address on the pad. *(MARCO goes behind the counter to look at the pad.)* It's the building on the corner.

MARCO. Yeah—right next door. *(He puts the pad down and comes from behind the counter looking at her, curiously.)* What're you doin' livin' in a place like that? In a neighborhood like this?

BETTY. Why not?

MARCO. Lemme put it this way—no family 'round here has got their own cook.

BETTY. That's why I'm here.

MARCO. Thank you. That clears up everything. *(returning to the ladder and painting)* So, you're gonna haveta get outta there soon. They're tearin' that building down an' the Addison Corporation is puttin' up a thirty story apartment house.

BETTY. A thirty-five story condominium. I don't know exactly when they start erecting this monster, but they said they would give me four weeks notice. You'll be having to leave here, too. They've bought this building. Why are you bothering to paint?

MARCO. Uh uh! We got an iron-bound lease which still has ten years to go. They can't budge us.

BETTY. I thought Addison was buying your lease.

MARCO. That's what they thought. Vinnie says they made a ridiculous offer. He spit in their eye. I'm gonna sell my half interest here to Vinnie 'cause I wanna get outta here. Vinnie can sell it to somebody who wants a little income without workin' his ass off.

BETTY. Your share should bring you quite a bit of money.

MARCO. Right. Vinnie's givin' me twelve an' a half grand. We figure, with a ten year lease, this place could bring twenty-five thousand.

BETTY. Is that all?

MARCO. Is that *all?* Where do ya think you are— Sardi's? Would ya like to take a guess as to how many times Mrs. Onassis has had lunch here?

BETTY. I just thought the property might ...

MARCO. *(interrupting)* Please! Let Vinnie do the thinking. He knows more about restaurants than anybody. He owns four ... all sea food joints ... very first class ... with banquettes an' lights on the table. The waiters and waitresses all got little sea horses engraved on their uniforms. Beautiful. Ever been to The Admiral?

BETTY. The Admiral?

MARCO. It's on Second Avenue near 53rd Street. Try to get in. I wish ya luck! He owns The Anchor an' The Shoreline, an' The Moby Dick. Vinnie's a millionaire. He drives a Mercedes, wears six hundred dollar suits an' his kids go to good schools. He'll be very happy to get twenty-five grand for this dump. I'm paintin' so maybe

he can unload it a little faster. He don't know I'm doin'
this. I'm gonna surprise him. *(He finishes painting, steps off
the ladder and looks at it.)* There. How does it look?

BETTY. *(looking at the wall)* It looks like a freshly painted
wall. What goes up there?

MARCO. What do you mean?

BETTY. *(crossing to behind the counter)* Haven't you got a
picture or a poster to hang there? It's awfully stark, don't
you think? *(BETTY picks up the coffee mugs and starts to wash
them in the sink below the counter.)*

MARCO. *(staring at the wall)* I had a picture of a lion on a
calendar, but I spilled paint on it. Screw it! The new
owner can put up what he likes. *(He turns to BETTY.)*
What're ya doin'?

BETTY. Washing the cups.

MARCO. You don't have to do that. C'mom!

BETTY. I love washing dishes. I found I love clean-
ing things.

MARCO. You *love* washing dishes?! You mean like
it's a hobby?

BETTY. I find it sort of remedial ... and please don't
look for comparisons with Lady Macbeth.

MARCO. Don't worry. *(He goes to the storage room.)* I got a
nice surprise for ya. *(He goes in to the store room and returns
with his hands loaded with a stack of dirty dishes.)* Look what we
got here!!

BETTY. Oh. I won't have time to do all those.

MARCO. *(setting the dishes down)* You don't have to do
any. I was just tryin' to make ya happy. *(Betty takes a dish
from the stack and washes it. MARCO finds a dish towel and
dries.)*

BETTY. What are you going to do when you leave here?

MARCO. I don't know. I got no plans.

BETTY. Don't you have any dreams? What would you like to do?

MARCO. I got what you could call the impossible dream. I would like to have a restaurant of my own— Italian, but smart ... fancy. The kind o' place Liz Smtih would write about. People like Sinatra would come in ... an' the governor ... maybe Woody Allen.

BETTY. Sounds terrific. Why is it impossible?

MARCO. 'Cause it takes a special kind of ability an' knowledge to run a restaurant an' I don't have that.

BETTY. Who says so?

MARCO. Vinnie.

BETTY. How does he know?

MARCO. He knows me inside out. Also he knows the restaurant business inside out. He was workin' in restaurants while I was still in diapers.

BETTY. Is he that much older than you?

MARCO. Seventeen years. I was an accident. No one was expectin' me to be born. Vinnie was more like my father than my brother an' if Vinnie tells you you ain't cut out for the restaurant business, if you're smart, you'll listen.

BETTY. And if you're smart, you can learn. Have you ever heard of The Restaurant School?

MARCO. No.

BETTY. There's one in Philadelphia ... a few, in fact and there must be some here.

MARCO. Ya mean they teach cookin'? I know how to cook.

BETTY. They teach *management*. You can learn all about licenses and taxes, budgeting and bookkeeping, customer and personnel psychology. They teach all about wines and liquors... how to prepare menus... advertising ... everything you need to know. *(MARCO sets down the plate he has been drying, comes down below the counter, thoughtfully.)*

MARCO. They really teach all that?

BETTY. *(joining him)* Marco, you can learn anything you have to know. God, if a man can learn to be a brain surgeon, he can learn to run a restaurant.

MARCO. How long does it take?

BETTY. I guess that depends on how many courses you take. The brother of a friend of mine went to the school because he decided one day he wanted to own a restaurant. He knew nothing about it. He's now in California with one of the best restaurants in Beverly Hills.

MARCO. An' he knew nothin' 'bout restaurants?

BETTY. Nothing. I've forgotten what he did before. Probably a brain surgeon.

MARCO. I like it! Yeah, I like it! *(He rushes to the pay phone, taking a coin from his pocket. He deposits the coin and dials.)*

BETTY. Who are you calling?

MARCO. *(into phone)* Yeah, Lou—I know it's The Admiral. Vinnie there?

BETTY. *(irritated)* Well, I guess there are some things you *can't* learn.

MARCO. *(As he speaks into phone, he becomes filled with anxiety and nervousness.)* Vinnie? It's me. Listen, I... uh... Oh, I'm sorry. Lou shoulda told me you're in a meeting. This'll only take a minute ... yeah, it's important. Yeah,

I'll make it fast. This lady is in here ... no, she lives next door in that building that's comin' down ... Yeah, she's still livin' there. Well, Vin, she told me that there's schools that teach everything ya haveta know 'bout runnin' a restaurant. They teach like wines an' liquor ... advertising ... I could learn *everything*. I thought ... ya know ... maybe I should look into it. *(He listens for a moment and his face clouds.)* Well ... it couldn't hurt, could it? Yeah ... I know, Vin but ... Yeah, I see. No, Vin, it don't go in one ear an' out the other, I just thought maybe ... But, Vin ... Vinnie? Vinnie? *(He looks at the receiver and hangs up the phone, shaken. He composes himself and avoids look-ing at BETTY who is watching him intently. MARCO stares at the left wall.)* I think you're right about that wall. It needs something.

BETTY. *(returning to the dishes and the washing)* Don't you think you ought to have another opinion.

MARCO. I don't need another opinion. I just talked to a specialist. He says I'd be throwin' out my money goin' to a school. He says ya learn by *doing*, not by *learning*. *(looking at the wall)* I wish I knew what to do 'bout that wall.

BETTY. Suppose you did know how to run a restaurant, could you afford one?

MARCO. No way! To open a place like I want—even with minimum renovations—we're talkin' 'bout a hundred grand. All I got is the twelve an' a half I'll have from my share o' this place.

BETTY. How about a loan from a bank?

MARCO. Banks don't give ya the whole thing. I'd need to go in with at least forty thousand o' my own.

BETTY. But isn't it possible to ...

MARCO. *(interrupting, angrily)* Drop it, will ya! I don't

wanta talk about it, anymore! I wish ya hadn't mentioned it in the first place. Vinnie's annoyed with me now.

BETTY. *(crossing to him)* You're afraid of Vinnie, aren't you?

MARCO. *(moving away from her, toward the store window)* What're you, *crazy?!* Yeah—must be all that hot water from doin' dishes ... it does somethin' to the brain.

BETTY. I've never heard of dish pan brains.

MARCO. I thank the good Lord I got someone like Vinnie to keep me from fallin' on my ass. I trust him more than anyone in the world. Ya know why? 'Cause he's Italian, an' so am I?

BETTY. *(moving closer to him)* You mean you wouldn't trust him so much if he were Norwegian?

MARCO. *(crossing right to get away from her)* Damn right! With Italian's, the family comes first. It's in our blood. Italian brothers are closer than any others—that goes for Norwegian, French, Chinese ... You wouldn't understand 'cause you're not Italian.

BETTY. Marco, It's very healthy of you to be proud of your heritage, but it's a mistake to think because you're Italian that you're better than anybody else. *(She turns and looks out of the store window.)*

MARCO. I didn't say I was better than anybody else. I just say that Italians are ... well, *special.* I feel special that I'm Italian, that's all. *(BETTY see something through the window. She turns to MARCO, alarmed.)*

BETTY. Marco, there's a man coming down the street. If he tries to come in here, don't let him. *(She rushes to the restroom.)*

MARCO. *(baffled)* What man? Who?

BETTY. Just get rid of him. I'll hide in here.

(BETTY exits into restroom. HENRY RITTER appears in the window. He is in his early thirties, handsome, affluent and cultured. HENRY looks through the window. MARCO looks back at him. HENRY moves to the door. MARCO rushes to the door to lock it. He is too late and HENRY opens the door.)

MARCO. Sorry—we're closed. Can't anybody read the sign?

HENRY. I don't want anything to eat. I just want to use your phone. I won't be a minute. *(Before MARCO can stop him, HENRY slides past him, crosses to phone, takes a coin from his pocket and deposits it.)*

MARCO. Could ya make it fast? Somebody might be tryin' to get me. *(He looks toward the restroom, nervously.)*

HENRY. This won't take long. *(HENRY dials, then hangs on the phone, impatiently, as MARCO steals furtive glances toward the restroom.)* Damn! No answer. *(He turns from the phone, facing the restroom, thinking.)*

MARCO. It's out of order.

HENRY. What is?

MARCO. You were lookin' at the john, weren't you?

HENRY. No. I was just thinking. *(MARCO takes HEN-RY'S arm and ushers him to the door.)*

MARCO. Well, don't think about the john 'cause it ain't workin'. Come back Tuesday. Nice to've met ya.

HENRY. Thank you for letting me use the phone.

(HENRY leaves the shop. MARCO watches through the window as HENRY passes out of view. MARCO leans forward to track

*HENRY'S movements as BETTY sticks her head out of the rest-
room door.)*

BETTY. Has he gone?

MARCO. He's gettin' in to a blue Ferrari. *(BETTY comes
out of the restroom.)* He needs air in the right rear tire.

BETTY. That's not all he needs.

MARCO. *(leaving the window)* Who is he?

BETTY. Nobody.

MARCO. Nobody? Everytime nobody walks by, you
gonna run an' hide in the toilet? Listen ... uh ... do you
owe money?

BETTY. It's nothing like that.

MARCO. I don't think he was even lookin' for you. He
just wanted to use the phone. Whoever he called
didn't answer.

BETTY. Of course not. I'm here. *(She crosses to the window
and looks out.)*

MARCO. He was callin' you?

BETTY. He's gone. *(She looks at the window seeing something of interest.)* He used to just drop in on me. I told him
never to do that without calling first. *(BETTY crosses to
behind the counter, finds a paper napkin and wets it.)*

MARCO. So, who is he?

BETTY. His full name is Henry Bancroft Ritter, the
third. He's an architect. He's one of the architects design-
ing the condominium and he comes down here every few
days to look at the property. *(She carries the wet napkin and a
few dry napkins toward the window.)*

MARCO. That's how ya met him?

BETTY. No, that's how I found out about the apartment.

MARCO. What're you doin'?!

BETTY. There are some fingerprint smudges on the window.

MARCO. Look, you don't have to do windows here. The dishes will be enough, thank you. We got a kid who comes and does the windows. *(BETTY crosses to behind the counter and drops the napkins in a waste bin.)* So, how'd ya meet Henry Ritter?

BETTY. I've known him forever. He and my brother went through school together.

MARCO. Seems like a nice fella. He's got nice manners—thanked me for the phone. Why'd ya hide?

BETTY. Because he'll tell my family that he saw Betty hanging around a coffee shop with some Dago kid.

MARCO. Hey! Don't use that word, Dago. It's insulting.

BETTY. I don't use that word.

MARCO. You just did.

BETTY. I was telling you what Henry will say.

MARCO. You don't like him, is that it?

BETTY. I don't really *dislike* him. I dislike what he stands for. We're a product of the same background—and that's not something I'm proud of.

MARCO. You mean your family? You don't like your family?

BETTY. Let's just say we're not close.

MARCO. *(amazed)* You're not close to your own mother and father?

BETTY. Marco, we're not Italian.

MARCO. Do you speak to each other?

BETTY. We speak, but we never *talk* The only way to get

my dad's attention is to commit a felony and come up before him for sentencing.

MARCO. And your mother? Does she do anything besides not cooking?

BETTY. She has her hair done a lot… and she serves on dozens of committees. Committees to fight alcohol and drug abuse and to benefit the handicapped and the destitute and victims of domestic abuse and so on and so on.

MARCO. So, she helps people. I think that's nice.

BETTY. It would be even nicer if she had ever met one person she's helped, but there is no fear of that … and please don't tell me it's the thought that counts.

MARCO. No … I was just thinkin' … I'd like to hear the other side o' the story.

BETTY. Oh, I can give you that, too. Betty was a rebellious child, inconsiderate and difficult to handle. I ran away from home when I was nine years old.

MARCO. Nine??!

BETTY. Uh huh. We went to The Barclay Hotel.

MARCO. What do ya mean "we"?

BETTY. My governess went with me.

MARCO. I'd o' taken the cook.

BETTY. No way. They couldn't live without a cook. Dad arranged for the best suite at the Barclay and they thought it was all too amusing. *(looking at her watch)* Damn! I've got to go now.

MARCO. No, don't go. It's early.

BETTY. *(crossing to pick up her bag)* I've got only half an hour. That let's the bus out. I'll have to cab it.

MARCO. *(trying to detain her)* If you're takin' a cab, ya got a little time. *(looking at the left wall)* I'd like to settle what to do with that wall before ya go. Maybe a nice picture. Hey! Your museum—do they ever loan out pictures, or rent?

BETTY. Only to other museums. Can you paint?

MARCO. Not a picture. I ain't artistic. It runs in the family.

BETTY. I have an idea. Nothing spectacular, but it will relieve the starkness and I think you might like it.

MARCO. Yeah? What?

BETTY. I'll let it be a surprise. I'll pick up some paint and do it after work. Will you be here this evening?

MARCO. *(growing excited)* Yeah, sure. Listen ... uh ... sit down for a minute. I wanna ask ya some questions. *(He seats her on a stool.)* Now, you said there's nothin' between you an' Henry Ritter ...

BETTY. Not from my side, anyway.

MARCO. Well ... uh ... are ya seein' anyone else? Anyone special?

BETTY. Special. You mean Italian?

MARCO. I mean—you know—steady?

BETTY. No.

MARCO. *(pacing, anxiously)* Lemme ask ya somethin' ... Do you think I got a good personality?

BETTY. It's certainly interesting.

MARCO. I'm not too bad lookin', would ya say?

BETTY. I'd say you were very nice looking.

MARCO. Yeah? Well ... uh ... if I was to ask you out ... ya know, dinner in some nice place and maybe dancin' after ... what would ya say?

BETTY. If you don't ask, you'll never know, will you?

MARCO. I don't like to ask a chick out 'less I know she's gonna say okay.

BETTY. I would never have dreamed you suffer from a fear of rejection.

MARCO. I don't suffer from nothin'. I'm just askin' a simple, every day question. Would you consider goin' out with me?

BETTY. I would certainly consider it *if* I were asked.

MARCO. So? Ya sayin' yes?

BETTY. So? You asking?

MARCO. Okay! I'm askin'!

BETTY. When?

MARCO. Tonight.

BETTY. I'd love it.

MARCO. Okay, that's settled. I wanna take ya some nice place uptown. How 'bout The Four Seasons?

BETTY. I'd much rather go to some cozy place around here.

MARCO. There's nothin' but slop joints 'round here. I wanna go someplace where I gotta wear a tie an' ya need a reservation.

BETTY. You know what I'd really like? I'd like to eat here and I'd like you to cook. You've been bragging so much about your cooking ... well, put up or shut up.

MARCO. Lady, you got it!

BETTY. Terrific! *(starting for the door)* I'll see you later.

MARCO. *(following her)* We'll have a good time, you'll see. I ain't intellectual, but I ain't stupid, either. You'd be surprised how much I know. Like ... uh ... can you name all the presidents?

BETTY. Of the United States?

MARCO. No, of Uganda! Of course the United States.

BETTY. No, I can't possibly name them all. Can you?

MARCO. Get a load o' this! *(He reels off the names, gasping for breath as he needs it.)* Washington, Adams, Jefferson, Madison, Monroe, Adams, Jackson, Van Buren, Harrison, Tyler, Polk, Taylor, Fillmore, Pierce, Buchanan, Lincoln, Johnson, Grant, Garfield, Arthur, Cleveland, Harrison, McKinley, Roosevelt, Taft, Wilson, Harding, Coolidge, Hoover, Roosevelt, Truman, Eisenhower, Kennedy, Johnson, Nixon, Ford, Carter, Reagan!! *(He takes a bow.)*

BETTY. You left out Hayes.

MARCO. I did not! Did I?

BETTY. You left out Rutherford B. Hayes. He comes between Grant and Garfield. He's the only one I can name because he was a cousin to my great great great great grandfather.

MARCO. *(bowled over)* You're related to Rutherford B. Hayes??!!

BETTY. So distantly, I'm not sure it counts.

MARCO. But ... bein' related to a president o' the United States of America ... That's gotta be goddamn wonderful!!

BETTY. Yes, Marco, it's wonderful. I never have to wait in line to see a movie. Taxis stop for me in the rain and repair men come running out on Saturdays to fix my refrigerator. *(opening the door)* I'll be back.

MARCO. Listen... you ain't had any lunch. Wanna grab a quick bite somewhere?

BETTY. I'll eat at the museum.

MARCO. You can eat in a museum?

BETTY. You can eat in this one. They have a nice lunchroom downstairs. I should be back a little after six.

MARCO. Ya won't forget, huh? Should I write it down for you?

BETTY. Don't worry ... just don't *you* forget to shop for dinner. (*BETTY exits. MARCO stands looking after her, admiringly. He closes the door and walks toward the counter, strutting and snapping his fingers. He stops, suddenly. A huge smile comes to his face as an idea strikes him. He rushes to the storage room and comes out putting on a windbreaker jacket. He* runs his fingers through his hair as he crosses to the telephone. He takes a coin from his pocket, deposits it and dials three digits.)

MARCO. (*into phone*) Information? I would like the number of the Metropolitan Museum Of Art ... 879-5000. Thanks. Yeah, I'm *havin'* a nice day. (*He hangs up. The coin is returned. He redeposits the coin and dials.*) Hello? Is this the Metropolitan Museum Of Art? Uh ... could you please tell me exactly where you're located?

CURTAIN

ACT TWO
Scene One

The same. Early that evening.

AT RISE: The blind on the shop window has been lowered, as has the shade on the front door. One of the small tables has been moved near center and set with a red and white checkered table cloth, a basket of bread, cutlery, wine glasses and votive candles. A large pot for cooking pasta can be seen on the stove as well as smaller pots. The left wall has now been sectioned in to three equal panels. The first panel has been painted green, the center panel remains white and the third panel is being painted red by BETTY, on the ladder and wearing an apron over the dress she has changed in to. She has a glass of red wine on the ladder. MARCO, wearing a shirt and gray flannel trousers, is seated on a stool behind the counter with a glass of wine and the bottle in front of him. He is studying a catalogue from the Metropolitan Museum.

MARCO. How many paintings ya suppose they got in that place?

BETTY. They own over a million pieces of art.

MARCO. Over a million?! So, I just saw a drop in the bucket.

BETTY. Not even that. You just saw a few of the Italians. I thought you'd like to start with the Italians ... Tintoretto ... Botticelli ...

MARCO. Ya gotta say one thing 'bout Italians—they don't just sing. How come I didn't see the Mona Lisa?

BETTY. It's in the Louvre in Paris.

MARCO. I guess the Met could buy it if they wanted it, huh? Aaanh, whadda they need it for?

BETTY. (finishes painting and comes down from the ladder) There! Finished! Come and look. (MARCO comes from behind the counter and joins BETTY. He looks at the wall and is clearly disappointed.)

MARCO. That's it??

BETTY. You don't like it.

MARCO. I thought you were gonna paint like a picture or somethin'.

BETTY. This is 'or somethin'. You must admit it breaks up all that unrelieved white.

MARCO. (His face lights up.) Hey!! Ya know what ya painted?

BETTY. (relieved) A breakthrough!

MARCO. (excited) Green, white an' red—that's the colors o' the Italian flag. You painted the Italian flag! It's terrific! I love it! I just love it! What made ya think o' that? Was it somethin' I said?

BETTY. It was *everything* you said.

MARCO. (shaking his head in awe) Beautiful ... just beautiful!

BETTY. All right. I've done my work for the evening. Now, let's sample yours.

MARCO. Dinner is served, signorina.

BETTY. *(removing her apron)* I'm just going to wash my hands.

MARCO. *(crossing to behind counter)* Yeah, go ahead. *(BETTY crosses to the restroom. We can see her washing her hands and wiping them on a paper towel from a dispenser. She fixes her hair. MARCO takes a bowl of salad from the refrigerator, pours dressing over it and tosses it. He divides the salad on to two plates. He uses a pot holder to take a pyrex dish of hot noodles from the oven. He tosses the noodles about with two forks and portions them on to two plates, then takes a small pot from the stove and spoons sauce over the pasta.*

BETTY. *(over action)* What are we having?

MARCO. Pasta an' salad.

BETTY. I'll be out in a minute to help.

MARCO. I don't need help. Listen I, ... uh ... I didn't put any garlic in the salad dressing, but it ain't too late. Ya want garlic?

BETTY. That depends on what we're doing later.

MARCO. I thought we might go dancin' ... an' then ... uh ... play it by ear.

BETTY. No garlic.

MARCO. *(grins and carries the salad plates to the table)* It's not too late to change your mind, ya know.

BETTY. About what?

MARCO. If you wanna go to The Four Seasons or some classy place. *(He returns to the counter.)*

BETTY. I like what we're doing, don't you?

MARCO. Oh, yeah. I like it fine. *(carrying the pasta to the table)* Ya don't haveta be ashamed to be seen with me. I know how to use the right fork an' spoon.

BETTY. *(Comes out of the restroom.)* Don't say stupid things like that. You're not stupid and don't pretend to be. *(She crosses to the table.)*

MARCO. *(pouring wine into the glasses)* I was only kiddin'. *(He rushes around the table to hold BETTY'S chair out for her. BETTY sits. MARCO, taking his seat and looking at the left wall.)* I hope I did as well by you as you did by me. I love that wall.

BETTY. *(eating her pasta)* Marco, this is wonderful ... I mean truly *wonderful.* This sauce is to die over!

MARCO. *(eating)* Highly not bad. It's my own sauce that I made up an' it's a secret, so don't ask for the recipe.

BETTY. What would I do with it?

MARCO. Yeah, that's right.

BETTY. If you can cook like this, then you *should* have your own restaurant.

MARCO. *(upset)* I told ya not to mention that again. What're ya tryin' to do—start trouble?

BETTY. *(insidiously)* What would it look like? What kind of decor?

MARCO. You wanna ruin the evening? Drop it, will ya?!!

BETTY. Red checkered table cloths with bread sticks on the table?

MARCO. How can you study higher education when you can't understand English?

BETTY. Candles stuck in Chianti bottles?

MARCO. No!! No candles stuck in Chianti bottles an' no checked table cloths. It would be elegant ... like sophisticated ... first class all the way. *(He rises and paces as he describes his dream restaurant.)* Maybe lace tablecloths with little pink lights on the table ... some guy playin' a violin walkin' around. There would be a lot o' chandeliers hangin' down. The waiters would wear smart uniforms with gold buttons an' gold braid ... an' the maitre d' would wear tails an' hand you a velvet menu. Ya know what I mean?

BETTY. Yes. You mean pretentious.

MARCO. Yeah, that's right. *(dreamily)* I want it to be pretentious. *(BETTY bursts out laughing. MARCO turns to her, angrily.)* Don't laugh at me!!

BETTY. *(Rises and goes to him.)* Marco, I'm sorry. I thought you meant to be funny. I guess you don't know the meaning of pretentious.

MARCO. If I make a mistake, correct me, but don't laugh at me. Ignorance is bliss, but it ain't funny. So, practice what you preach. What does pretentious mean?

BETTY. Putting on airs.

MARCO. Oh. An' I said I wanted ... *(He bursts out laughing.)* Yeah, that *is* funny. *(seriously)* Okay, you can laugh. Hey, I wanna take a picture o' that wall. *(He crosses to behind the counter, reaches down and brings up a camera case.)*

MARCO. *(crossing to the table)* I wanna take your picture ... an' I wanna take a picture o' that wall. *(He takes the camera out of the case.)* Vinnie gimme this camera. They call it the idiot camera.

BETTY. Why?

MARCO. 'Cause it's so easy to use. All you gotta do is aim an' snap. An idiot could use it. Ya wanna see some pictures I took? *(He takes a batch of pictures from the camera case, selects one and shows it to BETTY.)* This is a picture of the outside o' the shop.

BETTY. *(Looks at it as she finishes her food. She nods.)* Nice. Aren't you going to eat?

MARCO. *(selecting another picture)* Later.

BETTY. *(switching her empty plate with MARCO'S)* Mind if I take yours?

MARCO. Is it that good or you just can't wait to wash the dishes?

BETTY. A little of both.

MARCO. *(showing her the picture)* This is the outside o' the shop from across the street.

BETTY. Mm hmm.

MARCO. *(showing her another picture)* This is the outside o' the shop from across the street an' down to the left a little.

BETTY. Sweet. Don't you ever take pictures of anything but the shop?

MARCO. Yeah, sure. *(He selects another and hands it to her.)* This is a girl named Audrey. She usedta work here part time.

BETTY. *(Looks at the picture and hands it back to him.)* Marco, this is a terrible picture.

MARCO. *(studying the picture)* What do ya mean? It's in focus. It's clear.

BETTY. It's a dirty picture.

MARCO. It is not dirty!

BETTY. Indecent, then.

MARCO. Indecent? Why? She's wearin' a bra an' panties. You can't see nothin'.

BETTY. Marco, that picture is offensive and you shouldn't show it around. *(He returns to his chair and sits, studying the picture.)*

MARCO. Jesus! How many pictures did we see in the museum today where the broads were completely naked an' ya never said any o' them was dirty or indecent. This girl ain't even naked. I seen pictures of a painting o' some princess or somethin' where she's leanin' back against a lot o' pillows like this ... *(He clasps his hands behind his head and brings his legs together, raising them at an angle.)* ... an' she's stark naked. It's a famous picture—probably there in your museum. Go look at it an' tell me if that ain't indecent!

BETTY. You're thinking of the Naked Maja. It's a painting of the Duchess of Alba by Goya—and it's not in my museum. It's in the Prado in Madrid.

MARCO. So why is my picture dirty an' not that one?

BETTY. Because the Duchess of Alba is not wearing spiked heels and a garter belt and bending over winking at us between her legs.

MARCO. We thought that was cute.

BETTY. Cute is not art. *(She sees she has hurt his feelings. She goes to him.)* Come on, show me a nice picture.

MARCO. *(looking through the pictures, selects one and rises to show it to her)* Here's one you'll like ... nice, clean family picture. It's practically holy. That's Vinnie .. an' that's Vinnie's wife, Fran ... an' those are their two kids. Alicia is twelve an' Helena is eleven almost.

BETTY. You worship Vinnie, don't you?

MARCO. You don't understand that?

BETTY. Oh, yes. I'm capable of understanding something I've never experienced.

MARCO. He's always been great to me. Like when I was little an' he went on a trip somewhere, he never came back without a present—some kind o' game or toy. I remember when he used to come back, even before I'd say "hello," I'd say "What'd ya bring me?" It's the same today. Vinnie goes to Florida or the coast, when he comes back, I still say, "What'd ya bring me?"

BETTY. Greedly little thing, aren't you?

MARCO. *(grinning)* Yeah!

BETTY. *(picking up the camera)* Let me take your picture with the wall.

MARCO. *(crossing to the left wall)* Okay, then I wanna take yours. *(MARCO stands beside the ladder with his arms folded over his chest, beaming, proudly.)*

BETTY. *(looking in to camera)* Is there enough light?

MARCO. Yeah—that's extra fast film.

BETTY. *(snaps the picture)* That sould be nice.

MARCO. *(crossing to BETTY and taking the camera)* Did you get the whole wall in?

BETTY. *(crossing to ladder)* I don't know. I'm not an idiot. *(As MARCO looks in to the camera and moves about searching for the right angle, BETTY swings around so she is facing the ladder. She places one foot on the first rung, raises her skirt above her waist, pokes her fanny out, opens her mouth, seductively, and winks.*

MARCO. What the hell are ya doin"??!!

BETTY. Don't you think this is cute? I thought you'd like a cute picture. *(She wiggles her fanny.)*

MARCO. Cut that out. It's disgustin'! *(BETTY climbs the ladder and sits midway up, folding her hands in her lap and smiling, demurely.)* Yeah, that's better. Nice smile now. *(He *snaps the picture. MARCO rushes forward to help BETTY down the ladder. She jumps the last step and falls in to MARCO'S arms. BETTY waits for him to make a move, but he continues to stare into her eyes, uncertainly. Finally, BETTY slips her arms about his neck, pulls his face close and kisses him.)*

BETTY. Thank God I remembered your fear of rejection or we'd be standing here all night.

MARCO. I told ya—I don't have no fear o' rejection. I just was't sure what to do. You're different from girls I know.

BETTY. So it's a fear of Rutherford B. Hayes. *(MARCO kisses her again, passionately. They pull apart.)*

BETTY. What about our dinner?

MARCO. I'll freeze it for ya.

(He kisses here again. The phone rings. He pulls away and looks at the phone, filled with anxiety.)

MARCO. It's Vinnie.

BETTY. How do you know?

MARCO. What time is it?

BETTY. *(glancing at her watch)* Eight-thirty.

MARCO. It's Vinnie. He calls every night at closing time. *(He starts toward the phone.)*

BETTY. Marco!! *(He stops and turns.)* Don't answer that phone.

MARCO. It'll only take a minute.

BETTY. *(firmly)* If you answer that phone, I am leaving. *(She crosses and picks up her bag. She stands waiting for his decision. MARCO, a bundle of nerves, looks at the phone, then back at her.)* I mean it. *(Again, MARCO looks at the ringing phone, then at BETTY, confused and fraught with indecsion.*

CURTAIN

Scene Two

SCENE: The same. The next morning.

AT RISE: The tables and chairs have been set in their proper places. The ladder, the drop cloth and the paints are gone. The cooking utensils have been put away. Two used wine glasses and two used plates are on the counter. The shade on the front door is down as is the blind on the window. MARCO enters through the front door, using his key. He is wearing a fresh dress shirt, gray trousers and carrying a blazer over his shoulder. He is in a happy mood as he raises the shade on the door and then the blind on the window. He crosses to the storage room and hangs up his blazer. He turns the kettle on, then crosses to the left wall. He admires the wall and feels it to see if it is dry. He turns, quickly, and looks at the phone. He crosses to it, taking a coin from his pocket. He is filled with anticipation as he deposits the coin and dials.

MARCO. *(into phone)* Hi, Fran, it's me ... No, don't get Vinnie outta the shower, I wanna talk to you. It's 'bout tomorrow night... sure I'm comin'. Don't I always come to dinner Monday night? What I'd like to know is—

would it be okay if I like brought somebody with me? ... Her name is Betty Neal. No, you don't know her. No, Vinnie don't know her. Excuse me, Vinnie *doesn't* know her. She's a very good friend o' mine. I met her yesterday. She came in to the store yesterday an' we ... like got to know each other. She lives next door where they're gonna erect that condo. I'd really like to bring her with me tomorrow ... Well, I'd like her to meet the family ... Listen, Fran, just gimme an answer—yes or no, okay? *(excitedly)* Yeah? Hey, that's swell. I really appreciate it. Look, I'd like to ask ya one more small favor ... Would ya mind usin' that nice table cloth? The blue one with the matching napkins ... yeah ... looks nicer than the plastic mats ... an' maybe the kids could look nice, too. ya know what I mean. Thanks a million, Fran, you're one great broad. I'll call ya later an' let ya know if she can come.

(MARCO hangs up as the kettle whistles. He crosses to it and fixes a mug of coffee. BETTY appears at the door carrying a large shoulder bag. She looks at the sign in the door and raps.)

    MARCO. Come in!

(BETTY enters.)

Why ain't ya ... Why aren't you sleeping? It's Sunday.
    BETTY. *(setting her bag on the floor near the counter)* I woke up and you were gone. Where did you go?
    MARCO. I left a note on the pillow.
    BETTY. It just said, "Good morning." It wasn't even signed.

MARCO. I figured you'd know it was me. I ran home and changed and stopped by here to clean up a little.

BETTY. We cleaned up last night.

MARCO. We missed a couple o' things.

BETTY. *(starting to join him behind counter)* Oh, well, I'll take care of ...

MARCO. *(stopping her)* No, please sit down. I wanna talk to you.

BETTY. *(takes a seat at the end of the counter and takes MARCO'S coffee)* You sound so serious.

MARCO. Well, I am, yeah. Now, lemme ask you somethin'. What did ya think o' last night?

BETTY. What do you mean?

MARCO. Well ... did ya enjoy yourself?

BETTY. Oh, Marco, you're not going to ask me if you were good, are you?

MARCO. No. I know I was good. What I wanna know is ... would you wish to continue?

BETTY. Would I *wish* to continue??

MARCO. I mean go on seein' each other on a regular basis.

BETTY. I know what you mean. It's the phraseology that threw me. "Would you wish to continue" sounds like a head waiter talking.

MARCO. I'm tryin' to up my language. If you hear me make mistakes in grammar or pronounciation, go ahead an' correct me.

BETTY. Well, it's proNUNciation, if you really care.

MARCO. Yeah, I do. Thanks. Now, lemme ask ya somethin'. How would you feel about ... like ... uh ... some kind o' relationship?

BETTY. I'm not sure I understand.

MARCO. I mean you an' me ... seein' each other on a regular basis ... goin' together.

BETTY. Do you mean living together?

MARCO. No! I hardly know you. I wouldn't ask a thing like that!

BETTY. You know, you're not only law-abiding, but you're fiercely moral, aren't you?

MARCO. So? Anything wrong with that?

BETTY. No. It's like a breath of fresh air.

MARCO. I noticed you took a minute to think 'bout what I was saying.

BETTY. Yes, but I wasn't thinking of morality. I was thinking of closet space.

MARCO. So. What d'ya say?

BETTY. Well... I thought people were supposed to drift in to relationships.

MARCO. No. I don't drift. I like to know yes or no, on or off, stop or go.

BETTY. I'm certainly willing to try it. Why not?

MARCO. Okay, that's settled. You workin' today?

BETTY. No.

MARCO. *(comes from behind the counter to join her)* How 'bout a stroll in Central Park an' maybe grab somethin' to eat in the cafeteria there by the zoo?

BETTY. I'm sorry, Marco, I can't today. I have some books in my bag to return to a classmate and there was talk about lunch.

MARCO. Oh. That's okay. What's his name?

BETTY. His name?

MARCO. Your classmate.

BETTY. His name is Marilyn. On second thought, I'll just drop the books off and get out of lunch.

(HENRY RITTER appears in the window, heading for the door. MARCO sees him and flies toward the door).

MARCO. He's here again ... your friend.

(MARCO reaches the door too late. HENRY enters as BETTY crosses to behind the counter and starts washing dishes. HENRY crosses to phone with MARCO following.)

HENRY. Hi! Just going to use the phone again. *(He deposits a coin and dials. MARCO glances back at BETTY, nervously. BETTY shrugs.)*
BETTY. *(when HENRY has finished dialing)* Hello?
HENRY. Betty?
BETTY. Henry! How nice of you to call. *(HENRY looks at the receiver, then turns and sees BETTY. He hangs up the phone.)*
HENRY. For a moment there ... what are you doing here?
BETTY. At the moment, I am doing dishes. I also do a little painting. *(pointing to the left wall)* I did that.
MARCO. It's the Italian flag. *(HENRY is unimpressed.)*
BETTY. *(coming from behind counter)* Henry, this is Marco. Marco, Henry.
HENRY. We met yesterday.
MARCO. *(going behind counter)* Would you like a cup o' coffee, Henry?
BETTY. No. Henry can't stay. He's very busy. *(She sits at

the counter.) Good-bye, Henry.

HENRY. *(joining BETTY at counter)* I can manage a cup of coffee. Yes, I'd like one.

MARCO. Comin' right up. *(He fixes a cup of coffee.)*

BETTY. Marco works here, too.

MARCO. I own this place.

HENRY. Oh, then you're Mr Fabrizio.

MARCO. I'm Marco Fabrizio. *Mr.* Fabrizio is my brother. We're partners here.

BETTY. Why are you down here on Sunday?

HENRY. The head of the wrecking company asked me to meet him to see what sort of traffic problem we might encounter.

MARCO. *(placing HENRY'S coffee before him)* There ya go.

HENRY. Thanks very much. *(He raises his mug as if to toast.)* Well—good morning, everybody. *(He sips the coffee.)*

MARCO. So ... uh ... tell me, Henry, when does you erection start? *(HENRY chokes on his coffee, then catches his breath.)*

HENRY. Sorry. You were asking about my ...

MARCO. The condominium. When does it go up?

HENRY. *(to BETTY)* Why does he make everything sound dirty?

BETTY. Why don't you ask him? He's standing right there.

HENRY. *(turning to MARCO and smiling, apologetically)* Well, the wreckers should start in about six weeks. We were held up, as you know, because ...

BETTY. *(jumping up and interrupting, quickly)* Oh, Henry,

it's Sunday! Please don't talk about your business ... or anyone else's.

HENRY. He asked me when ...

BETTY. I know—and I'm asking you to talk about something else. Do you mind?

HENRY. What's the matter with you? You're awfully jumpy. *(looking around)* What are you doing here, anyway?

BETTY. Just hanging around.

HENRY. *(gulps down his coffee and rises)* I was able to get a table at Elaine's tonight. Eight o'clock. I hope you'll be in a better mood.

BETTY. I'm sorry. I can't make it tonight.

HENRY. We had a date.

BETTY. It was tentative. I said check with me Sunday morning.

HENRY. All right, it's Sunday morning and I'm checking.

BETTY. I've made another date. I'm sorry.

HENRY. You should be. You've ruined my evening.

BETTY. You can ask someone else.

HENRY. I don't want to ask someone else. No problem ... I'm sure Elaine will be happy to have the table.

MARCO. Elaine's! I read about that place all the time.

BETTY. *(to MARCO, sharply)* You want to go with him?!

MARCO. No, I'm just sayin' ... *(to HENRY)* So, what about your dinner?

HENRY. What about it?

MARCO. You got a cook—or someone to make your

dinner. Can *you* cook?

HENRY. I have no help on Sundays ... *(smiling at BETTY)* ... especially from my friends. And, no, I don't cook.

MARCO. So, what're ya gonna do for dinner?

BETTY. What difference does it make?

MARCO. Ain't it enough the man's evening is ruined? He don't haveta starve, too. *(to HENRY)* You got any leftovers? Cold chicken or ham?

HENRY. No, but thank you for caring, Marco. I'll stop somewhere and get somethig.

MARCO. It's Sunday. Not much open. Just hold everything. I can help ya out. *(He picks up the pad and pencil.)* Tell me if ya hear anything you like. *(reading from the pad)* Chicken cacciatore with spaghetti ... Lasagne with meat sauce ... Chicken paprikash with noodles.

HENRY. *(to BETTY)* Sounds like your food.

BETTY. It is. My fridge broke down. *(to MARCO)* He likes creamed chipped beef.

MARCO. *(to HENRY)* Yeah? Well, we got two o'those. They're yours. *(He opens the freezer, digs down and brings up two boxes.)* Here we are! Just follow the instructions on the box. Very simple.

HENRY. Thanks very much.

MARCO. You're all set. *(looking at the pad)* Let's see ... okay, we cross off two creamed cipped beefs. *(He crosses them off, then pushes the pad and pencil over the counter to BETTY.)* Would ya please initial that? *(As BETTY initials the pad, MARCO searches under the counter and around the shelves behind him.)*

BETTY. What are you looking for?

MARCO. A bag. I'm outta bags. *(He crosses to the door.)* I'll get some. It won't take long.

BETTY. Don't leave. He doesn't need a bag.

MARCO. Sure he needs a bag. The stuff is ice cold.

HENRY. Of course I need a bag.

MARCO. Kaufman's drugstore is open. My friend, Merv, is the counterman. He's got those nice bags that keep things cold.

BETTY. Marco, don't leave ...

MARCO. An' ya could have a little talk while I'm gone. Be right back.

HENRY. I appreciate everything you're doing, Marco. *(MARCO exits. BETTY stands glaring at HENRY who is smiling at her like a Chesire cat.)* I am crazy about Marco!

BETTY. Henry, I want you to get out of here right now!

HENRY. I can't leave without my creamed chipped beef ... and I must wait for the bag ... and I can't leave without saying goodbye to Marco.

BETTY. *(hotly)* Oh, stop being arch and supercilious. I know what you're thinking! What is Betty doing here with this gorilla? Well, let me tell you he is not a gorilla. If he is an animal, he is a panther, an eagle. If the world comes crashing down tomorrow, Marco will survive. You and I will not!

HENRY. *(crossing to her)* Don't put words in to my mouth and don't put thoughts in to my head. On very short aquaintance he strikes me as a considerate man ... a good person.

BETTY. But not good enough for me, is that it?

HENRY. Or maybe you're not good enough for him.

The point is that you're worlds apart. The point is that you keep making the same mistake over and over.

BETTY. *(crosses to behind the counter picks up HENRY'S coffee cup and washes it)* Why do you feel you have the right to talk to me this way?

HENRY. I love you. You know that.

BETTY. But I don't love you and you know *that.*

HENRY. You did once.

BETTY. Please, not that again. All right, you were the first man I went to bed with. It wasn't a bed, was it? It was a sofa in our pool house. You were kind and gentle and I will be eternally grateful, but the penetration of my body does not entitle you to invasion of my privacy.

HENRY. No matter what you say now, you were in love with me that night.

BETTY. No, I wasn't. I did it for the experience. I wanted to know what it was like because Cissie Coleridge was raving about it. And it was very exciting—like getting my first driver's license. It had nothing to do with love. *(She crosses toward the window to move away from HENRY. He follows.)*

HENRY. You could love me, but I have one gigantic strike against me: I am acceptable to your family.

BETTY. Acceptable?! They adore you.

HENRY. And that throws me right out of the ball park.

BETTY. Please let's drop it.

HENRY. Look at the men you've been attracted to over the past few years—the truck driver.

BETTY. He was very nice. He gave me a lift home when my car broke down.

HENRY. The bartender at The Warwick.

BETTY. He made wonderful whiskey sours.

HENRY. The garage mechanic. *(Betty turns and glares at him, sharply.)* Yes, I knew about that one, too.

BETTY. All right, and then there was the butcher, the baker and the candlestick maker.

HENRY. But you never marry any of them.

BETTY. I'd like to finish school first.

HENRY. No, it's some primal instinct that tells you it wouldn't work.

BETTY. What instinct tells you that marriage with you would work?

HENRY. It certainly has a better chance. We've grown up eating the same food, reading the same books, speaking the same language. That sounds like marriage to me.

BETTY. To me it sounds as though one of us isn't necessary. Face it, Henry, we're redundant. *(She crosses left, he follows.)*

HENRY. Betty, we know that most kids go through a period of malcontent with the family's values and traditions, but they grow out of it. Not you. You carry adolescent rebellion to heights no one has ever dreamed of ... and you're going to wind up hurting everyone in sight.

BETTY. I am capable of taking care of myself.

HENRY. I wasn't thinking of you. I was thinking of the guy you finally marry—the truck driver or the bartender ... or let's say Marco. Who will your friends be? Cissie Coleridge? Babs and Carter Maddox? Mimsy and Chuck Porter? Can you really see them with Marco? No. Well, maybe his friends will be your friends. Merv, the counterman at Kaufman's drugstore. It won't work, Betty. You can't change what you are. You've got eduction, breeding ... all that rich, cultivated blood flowing through your veins. You can't hide it. You can't even suppress it. *(She turns to him, deeply upset. She tries to speak, but can think of nothing to say.)* A Marco Fabrizio can't live with all that. Once the passion dies down— it does, you know— he'll be hurt by it.

(We see MARCO returning through the window.)

HENRY. First hurt, then hate.

(MARCO enters. He is aware of tension. He turns cheerful, waving the paper bag.)

MARCO. I got 'em awright!
HENRY. *(turns BETTY to him and kisses her, gently, on the cheek)* For God's sake, for *your* sake, grow up, Betty.

(MARCO crosses to behind the counter and puts the food boxes into a bag.)

MARCO. *(holding up the bag)* Here y'are. Enjoy!

(HENRY crosses to the counter and takes the bag. He shakes hands with MARCO.)

HENRY. Thanks. I'm very glad to have met you, Marco. Take care of yourself.

MARCO. Yeah, you too.

(HENRY crosses to the door, stops to look at BETTY. She looks at him. HENRY smiles at her and exits.)

MARCO. You okay?

(BETTY pulls herself out of her thoughts, turns to him and smiles.)

BETTY. Of course. Tell me something—why did you give Henry the food?

MARCO. *(coming from behind the counter)* Hey, I'll replace it. I didn't think you'd mind.

BETTY. I don't mind. I just want to know why.

MARCO. Well ... I felt like partly responsible for ruining his evening. This way, at least, I'll know he's gonna eat. I think he woulda done the same for me. He's a nice guy.

BETTY. Marco, don't be so damned trusting. Don't trust anyone—including me!

(VINNIE FABRIZIO appears in the window, heading for the door. He is carrying a large manila envelope under his arm.)

MARCO. What do you mean by that?

(VINNIE enters the shop, smiling.)

VINNIE. Hey!! *(MARCO turns and looks at VINNIE.)*

MARCO. *(excited)* It's Vinnie! *(He rushes to him with uncon-*

scious apprehension.) Hiya, Vin!!

(As MARCO and VINNIE embrace, BETTY moves up to the counter and sits on the last stool.)

VINNIE. Surprised, huh?

MARCO. What're ya doin' down here?

VINNIE. *(pinching MARCO'S cheek)* Visiting my little brother, what else?

MARCO. *(to BETTY)* This is Vinnie, I been tellin' ya 'bout. *(to VINNIE)* I would like you to meet my friend, Betty Neal. *(VINNIE and BETTY eye each other, coolly.)*

BETTY. How do you do?

VINNIE. Please to meet you. *(sniffing)* I smell paint.

MARCO. Yeah, I been paintin' the place. I wanted to surprise you. Wanna see somethin' sensational? *(indicating the left wall)* Look at that.

VINNIE. *(after a long look)* Well, what have we here— Gucci's?

MARCO. It's the Italian flag.

VINNIE. Nice—but people come in here to eat, not to salute.

BETTY. It was my idea. I did it.

VINNIE. *(rubbing his stomach which is causing him discomfort)* A place like this should be white. Why? Because white looks clean.

BETTY. It also looks antiseptic.

VINNIE. So? Antiseptic is clean, right?

MARCO. Vinnie knows 'bout these things.

VINNIE. *(to MARCO)* Why the hell are you painting here, anyway?

MARCO. I thought if I freshened it up a little, it might sell quicker.

VINNIE. Kid, anybody buying a place like this ain't buying it for the decor. They want decor, they buy La Caravelle or The Rainbow Room. *(VINNIE takes a seat at the opposite end of the counter from BETTY as MARCO goes behine the counter.)*

MARCO. *(seeing VINNIE rub his stomach)* Why ya rubbin' your stomach? Ya got pain.

VINNIE. It's nothing. I called you last night. You weren't home. Youweren't here.

MARCO. Well, I was ... uh ...

BETTY. He was out with me.

VINNIE. I see. I came by yesterday afternoon. The place was locked, the shades down. Since when do you close on Saturday?

MARCO. I took the afternoon off. The place was closed for paintin', anyway.

VINNIE. Where were you?

MARCO. I was at the Metropolitan Museum Of Art.

VINNIE. *(after a long, hard stare)* You don't want to tell me where you were, don't tell me.

MARCO. That's where I was. I swear.

VINNIE. You don't even know what city The Metropolitan Museum is in.

BETTY. He was there with me.

VINNIE. Oh ... with you again. *(to MARCO)* What were you doing there?

MARCO. Looking at pictures. Beautiful! I never saw so many beautiful pictures in one place.

VINNIE. *(rubbing his stomach and grimacing)* Give me

something. What've you got?

MARCO. Coffee? Tea?

VINNIE. No. I got gas. Got any Brioschi?

MARCO. Sure. *(MARCO reaches under the counter and brings up a bottle of Brioschi. He puts a tablespoon into a glass of water and sets it on the counter for VINNIE. Over the action above.)* Ya ever been to The Metropolitan Museum Of Art

VINNIE. Yeah, I been there.

MARCO. Ya never told me. When?

VINNIE. I drive by every day.

MARCO. I mean inside.

VINNIE. Look, kid, when you're running four restaurants, you won't have time to go inside. *(He drinks the Brioschi in one long gulp.)* How long you been closed?

MARCO. Since Thursday.

VINNIE. Since Thursday! Jesus! You don't need the godamn paint. You need the customers. You close a place like this even for a few days, you lose your regulars. They become regulars at the coffee shop around the corner because it's open. Don't you ever use your head?

BETTY. *(rises, uncomfortable)* I think I'd better go now.

MARCO. No, No! Don't leave yet. Would ya like some Brioschi? It's good for ya. Takes care o' headaches, flu, indigestion—even hangovers.

BETTY. I thought chicken soup did all that.

MARCO. For the Jews. For Italians, Brioschi.

VINNIE. *(to BETTY)* You Jewish?

BETTY. No. You don't have to be Jewish to like chicken soup.

VINNIE. If you don't mind me asking, what are you?

BETTY. Presbyterian.

VINNIE. I see. Then you're not Catholic.

BETTY. I don't think you can be both. Is not being Catholic a mark against me?

VINNIE. That depends on what you're trying out for. I can see you got other things going for you. You're a very pretty girl.

MARCO. *(to BETTY, anxiuosly)* He meant that as a compliment.

VINNIE. So, you live next door.

BETTY. Until they tear it down.

VINNIE. I thought everybody was out of there.

BETTY. I'm still there.

VINNIE. Do the Addison people come around much?

BETTY. I don't know. I mail the rent in.

MARCO. Guess who was just here? The architect who's working on the condo.

VINNIE. Yeah? What did he want?

MARCO. He stopped in to see Betty.

VINNIE. Everybody comes in but customers. Did he talk about the project?

MARCO. Not to me.

BETTY. *(pointedly)* He's talked about it to me. He's told me just about everything. If you want to know anything about the project, Vinnie, just ask me.

VINNIE. I'll remember that, but right now there's something else I'd like to know. I can tell, Betty, that you're a girl with education ... from a good background ... so ... uh ... why you hanging around with the kid here?

MARCO. What the hell kind o' question is that? What

am I, chopped liver?

VINNIE. *(ignoring MARCO)* I would expect a girl like you to be with doctors or lawyers ... maybe architects. It's hard for me to put you and the kid together.

BETTY. Why do you call him "the kid"?

VINNIE. It' short for kid brother.

MARCO. It's like a nickname. I don't mind that.

BETTY. You should.

VINNIE. Betty, please understand I got nothing against you. I'm just curious to find out what you and my brother have in common, that's all.

BETTY. Maybe it's chemistry. The chemistry between us is just right.

VINNIE. What does that mean? You got the same blood type?

BETTY. Do you ask these questions of every girl "the kid" goes out with?

MARCO. Cut the questions, Vin. When there's somethin' to tell ya, I'll tell ya. You won't have to ask.

VINNIE. You don't ask questions, you don't learn. I've got your interests at heart. Don't you undertand that? *(He smiles at MARCO and crosses to the counter.)* Here—let me show you how I got your interests at heart. *(He opens the manila envelope, takes out a batch of legal papers with a check clipped to the top. He takes the check and waves it in front of Marco's face.)* Here—now maybe you'll know what I'm talking about.

MARCO. *(takes the check and glances at it, quickly)* Hey! It's my check for my share o' this place. The papers ready?

VINNIE. *(holding up the contracts)* Becker delivered them

yesterday. That's why I came down here. That's why I was trying to get you on the phone. Look at the check again, will you?

MARCO. *(studies the check, then looks at VINNIE, astonished)* It says twenty-five thousand.

VINNIE. The kid can read. I'm throwing in my share.

MARCO. Aw, c'mon! No, I can't let ya do that.

VINNIE. Don't tell me what I can do and what I can't do. That's what mom and pop would've wanted.

MARCO. I don't know what to say. *(He hugs VINNIE.)* Jesus, Vin!! *(He shows the check to BETTY.)* Look at that. Ya see what I mean 'bout havin' an Italian brother?

BETTY. Is that enough to open your own restaurant?

MARCO. No, of course not. *(He grimaces and holds up his hands to BETTY to warn her to be quiet.)*

VINNIE. Oh, Jesus, don't start with your restaurant again!! I told you never to mention it!

BETTY. He didn't mention it. I did.

VINNIE. Why? What's it to you?

BETTY. I'm an ombudsman.

VINNIE. Well, why don't you go back there—where you belong? You're encouraging him in something that not only you know nothing about, but neither does he. I got four restaurants—all successful. Why? A combination of hard work and know-how. Nice places where familes come with children. Marco don't want that kind of operation. He wants a chi-chi place where the elite meet to eat. He wants to read about his place in the columns.

MARCO. Yeah, I'd like a place important people would

come to, but I never said it had to be that or nothin'.

VINNIE. You do what I tell you. Drop that check in the bank and leave it there. It'll be a cushion 'til you get into something permanent. *(placing the papers in front of MARCO)* Here are three copies of the agreement. You want to sign them or you want to go into business with Betty?

MARCO. Okay, okay—got a pen?

VINNIE. *(feeling his pockets)* No.

MARCO. *(to BETTY)* Got a pen?

BETTY. Probably. *(She crosses to her bag.)*

MARCO. I still think ya givin' me too much. Did ya talk to Fran 'bout it?

VINNIE. I want to help my brother, I don't need my wife's permission.

(BETTY, with her back to the men, reaches in to her bag, brings up a pen, looks at it for a moment, then lets it fall back in to the bag.)

BETTY. Sorry. I could have sworn I had one.

VINNIE. *(to MARCO)* Take them home and sign them and bring them when you come tomorrow night. *(He looks at BETTY.)* Tell me something, Betty. You speak Italian?

BETTY. Not really. Just sort of menu Itlian.

VINNIE. *(to MARCO, gesturing with his head toward the door)* Manda la via. Voglio parlarti.

MARCO. *(irritated)* Non e' gusto!

BETTY. I'd better get over to Marilyn's.

VINNIE. I thought you don't speak Italian.

BETTY. I know what this means ... *(She imitates VIN-NIE'S gesture.)* ... in any language.

MARCO. *(rushing to her)* Hey, hold it!

BETTY. Marco, I have to go.

MARCO. We had a date.

BETTY. I had a date with Marilyn first. On second thought, she may have cooked something and ...

MARCO. Wait just one minute, please. When ya walked in before ya said you were goin' to drop books off and lunch with Marilyn. Then you said, "On second thought I can get out of it." So, now we're up to your third thought. How many do ya need?

BETTY. A lot. *(to VINNIE)* Good-bye, Vinnie. *(She opens the door.)*

MARCO. *(holding the door)* Listen, come back as soon as ya finish. I'll be right here. I'll be waiting.

BETTY. No, please don't wait for me. *(Betty exits, quickly. MARCO closes the door and watches her pass the store window.)*

VINNIE. Lovely girl.

MARCO. *(turning to VINNIE, hotly)* Why were ya so goddamn rude, Vinnie? Why did ya tell me to get rid o' her— and in *Italian?*

VINNIE. I want to talk to you alone.

MARCO. So, why didn't ya say that. In *English?*

VINNIE. She was ready to leave. Couldn't you see that? She was leaving and it had nothing to do with me.

MARCO. Yeah, I think it did have something to do with you.

VINNIE. Come on, let's get outta here. I'll buy you a nice lunch.

MARCO. I don't want to go anywhere.

VINNIE. Marco, she's not coming back.

MARCO. Yes, she is. You don't know her. I know her an' I'm tellin' ya she'll be back. *You* leave, Vin. Tell ya the truth, I'd rather you were not here when she comes in.

VINNIE. You in love with her?

MARCO. C'mon! I only met her yesterday. Why don't ya ask me if we're gettin' a divorce? That makes as much sense as your question.

VINNIE. Fran told me you called and asked if you could bring her to dinner. You never brought a girl to dinner before. Look, nobody knows you better than me. You're a sensitive kid. You got a very romantic naure. If there was such a thing as love *before* first sight, that would be you. I just don't want to see you get stepped on, that's all. Betty is a girl with class and a college education. You don't even have a high school diploma.

MARCO. I'll tell ya somethin' that might surprise ya. Betty thinks I got a very good mind.

VINNIE. What did you do—name the presidents?

MARCO. It wasn't only that. She says I could be more than street smart. She makes me wanna be more! I wanna be able to speak better and maybe mix with better people.

VINNIE. Like Betty.

MARCO. Lemme tell ya a little 'bout Betty. Aside from bein' smart, she comes from a very important family. Her father is a judge an' ya ever heard o' Rutherford B. Hayes?

VINNIE. One of you presidents?

MARCO. He was the nineteenth president of the United States of America—an' he is a descendant of hers!!

VINNIE. You got a lot of respect for this girl, right?

MARCO. Of course. She ain't your every day Bimbo.

VINNIE. Remember what you said to me—at least a hundred times?

MARCO. Tell me what you're talkin' about, maybe I'll remember.

VINNIE. How many times did you say to me, "When I meet a girl I respect, I'll marry her.

MARCO. So?

VINNIE. That's what I'm asking you—*so??*

MARCO. She likes me—in spite of all the differences. She knows I'm not educated. she knows I'm not polished. I never tried to hide that. Still—she likes me.

VINNIE. All right, now you listen to me—because I promised mom and pop that I'd look out for you. There are thousands of beautiful Italian girls put there ... nice Catholic girls. Find one. Find a girl who's not smarter than you, then you'll have a marriage. A marriage has to be between equals. Look at me and Fran.

MARCO. Okay. Okay, look at you an' Fran. Fran went to college. You didn't.

VINNIE. She went for two years. She learned nothing. That makes us equal.

MARCO. Lemme ask ya somethin' ... if your marriage is so great how come you're foolin' 'round with Tina?

VINNIE. Tina?

MARCO. Yeah, Tina. Your bookkeeper.

VINNIE. Who said I'm fooling around with her?

MARCO. What difference does it make who said? It's true. So how come you're bangin' Tina if your marriage is so wonderful?

VINNIE. You're talking about an entirely different situation. In the first place, Tina is Italian.

MARCO. Oooooh, that makes it okay, huh? *(throwing up his hands)* Jesus! Vinnie! You always cease to amaze me!

VINNIE. Let me tell you something—Tina's got brains, too. She reads books, does crossword puzzles, goes to foreign movies. She's kind of like Betty, but I don't love her. I love Fran.

MARCO. Too bad Fran don't know how lucky she is.

VINNIE. Look, I've been around a lot longer than you—and in a lot of different circles, too. I'm telling you the whole time Betty was here, she was feeling superior to us.

MARCO. She is superior to us. Listen to how nice she speaks ...

VINNIE. I'm not talking about education. I am talking about intolerance. If you were a professor at Harvard, you'd be that *Italian* professor at Harvard.

MARCO. Betty don't think like that. The trouble with you is you never knew a girl like Betty.

VINNIE. *(stares at MARCO for a moment)* I'm going to tell you something I have never told anyone. I want you to listen carefully, because I am never going to tell it again... and I want you to understand. Before I ever knew Fran— I was about your age—I was in love with a girl named Laura Barnes. You wouldn't remember her. You were six, maybe seven at the time. She was top class all the way. She was beautiful ... worked as a fashion editor on a smart magazine. We were in love. The kind of love where you get dizzy just looking at each other. We went together nearly a year and were planning to get married. One night we had a fight. Today I can't remember how it started or what it was about, even, but it was a class A fight ... championship. She started calling me names. she called me a dirty wop ... a lousy guinea ... a Dago son of a bitch. I hit her. I hit her so hard I nearly broke her jaw. A few weeks later we tried to make up, but it was no good because by that time I hated her. Why? Because she made me feel ashamed of what I was ... what I came from. Do you understand what I'm telling you?

MARCO. I understand, but I'm tellin' you Betty ain't that kind o' girl.

VINNIE. Laura Barnes wasn't that kind of girl. they're never that kind of girl until you have a fight, then they're all that kind of girl. These girls are filled with intolerance and prejudice. it comes with the birth certificate.

MARCO. What you're sayin' 'bout *them*—ain't that intolerance and prejudice?

VINNIE. No, it's common sense. Thank your lucky stars that Betty took herself a walk.

MARCO. *(firmly)* She's comin' back.

VINNIE. Then you take yourself a walk! Come on, let's go up and eat. This place is depressing.

MARCO. I gotta finish paintin' the trim.

VINNIE. You can do that tomorrow.

MARCO. Vinnie, I don't wanna go anywhere. I am stayin' right here. Okay?

VINNIE. I'm not going to let you sit here feeling sorry for yourself. You should be out celebrating!

(BETTY appears in the window. She looks in, uncertainly.)

MARCO. There she is! I told ya, didn't I? Ya smart as hell, Vin, but ya don't know everything. *(MARCO starts for the door. VINNIE grabs his arm and stops him.)*

VINNIE. When she walks in here, you put an end to it. The longer you wait, the harder it is. Do it quick and clean. That way nobody gets hurt.

(MARCO breaks away and goes to the door as BETTY enters the shop. MARCO looks at her for a moment, trying to understand why she seems tense.)

MARCO. So? Ya didn't stay for lunch?

BETTY. I didn't go to Marilyn's. *(Her attention is now fixed on VINNIE.)* I just walked around ... and I decided to come back. Sorry, Vinnie—you win some, you lose some.

VINNIE. Why don't you just leave? Wouldn't that be better for everybody? Think about it.

MARCO. *(confused)* Why should she leave? Think about what?

BETTY. About whether or not I should tell you about Vinnie's deal with Addison Corporation.

(VINNIE moves to the window and stares out.)

MARCO. What the hell are you talking about?

BETTY. Your lease here is the one thing that's been holding up construction of the condo. The Addison people offered Vinnie fifty thousand for the lease. Vinnie held out for two hundred and fifty. They settled a few days ago for one hundred and eighty thousand.

MARCO. A hundred and eighty thousand for this dump? Oh, sure!!

BETTY. They need this space. A hundred and eighty thousand is petty cash for a company spending twenty-seven million to put up a building. Vinnie's twenty-five thousand to you is hardly magnanimous when you realize he's pocketing a hundred and fifty-five thousand!

MARCO. I don't believe it. How would you know?

BETTY. Henry Ritter told me. He started to talk about it when he was here, but I stopped him.

MARCO. Ya know what I think? I think that you are crazy. He's my brother, for criisake!! *(Smiling, he turns to VINNIE.)* Hey, Vin, tell her she's got the whole thing ... *(VINNIE stands staring out. He can not face MARCO. MARCO stares at VINNIE, his smile fading to a look of disbelief, followed by insane anger. He lunges at VINNIE, grabbing him by the throat.)* Ya goddamn son of a bitch!!

(VINNIE struggles with MARCO. BETTY rushes over and pulls MARCO away from VINNIE.)

BETTY. Marco, stop it! Don't be an animal!

MARCO. *(screaming at VINNIE)* You lousy bastard! I can't believe what I just heard!

BETTY. Cool it, Marco!!

MARCO. Cool it??!! Sure, why don't we all sit down an'

have tea?! *(to VINNIE)* Why?! WHY?!! You got all the bread in the world, for criisake! I don't have a nickel. All my life I believed ya when ya said, "I'm your brother. I love ya. I'll never steer ya wrong. Italian brothers look out for each other." You said all that, didn't ya? So, a chance comes along to rip me off an' what happens? We stop bein' Italian? I always looked up to you like you were a god. You're nothin' but a common thief! No wonder that that Laura called you a dirty wop an' a lousy Dago. Ya musta done somethin' really beautiful to her to make her wanna hurt ya like that. Lemme tell ya somethin'—I'm on *her* side! Right now I'm tryin' to think o' some names that'll rip your guts out!

(VINNIE has been listening to this, looking at MARCO in astonishment.)

VINNIE. Are you crazy? Are you out of your goddamn mind?!! Did you just tell me that I am stealing your money?!!

MARCO. *(waving VINNIE'S check)* This check is sixty-five thousand short. What do you call it—borrowing?

VINNIE. *(shaking his head)* Well, this beats everything. *(He turns to BETTY.)* I never thought I would live to see the day that my brother would call me a thief.

BETTY. The check *is* short.

MARCO. And undernourished!

VINNIE. *(to MARCO)* You think I'm keeping your money? That's what you think?

MARCO. Damn right!

VINNIE. *(pointing to the phone)* I want you to go to that

phone and call my lawyer. I want you to call Mike Becker right now and ask him about your sixty-five thousand. Go ahead—He'll tell you where your money is going.

MARCO. I don't wanna call Mike Becker. You tell me.

VINNIE. That money is going into a trust for you. It'll earn interest, but you can't touch the principal.

MARCO. Till when?

VINNIE. Till I think you're man enough to handle it.

MARCO. You mean when I grow up, don't ya? You know when I'm gonna grow up, Vinnie? Over your dead body, that's when!

VINNIE. If you had that money now, you'd piss it away in two months. You'd invest in some broken down restaurant and in two months you'd be flat on your ass!

MARCO. Don't ya think ya shoulda discussed it with me?

VINNIE. No! You would only argue like you're doing now. I know what I'm doing.

MARCO. But I don't like what you're doin'. I don't want my money in a trust. I want it right here in my pocket... an' if I wanna invest it in a restaurant, I will.

VINNIE. Sure! Just what New York needs is another new restaurant—especially one from you! You know nothing about it. *(to BETTY)* Can you see him going down to the fish market at six in the morning to pick out fresh fish?

BETTY. I can't see anybody doing that, but if it has to be done, Marco can do it. I think he can do anything he puts his mind to.

VINNIE. Why don't you stay out of this?

BETTY. I was staying out. You brought me in.

MARCO. Vinnie, the truth of the fact is the money belongs to me an' if I wanna piss it away, you got no right to stop me. I don't tell you not to piss your money away on six hundred dollar suits an' private schools for the kids an' driving a Mercedes ... not to mention Fran's perfume and jewelry ... *(turning to BETTY)* Why don't ya ask him 'bout the fur jacket for Tina?

BETTY. *(to VINNIE)* What about the fur jacket—and who is Tina?

MARCO. His bookkeeper ... among other things.

VINNIE. That jacket was just a Christmas bonus. Cost nothing. It was fun fur.

MARCO. Yeah—you had the fun an' she got the fur! *(He picks up the check and papers and stuffs them into the manila envelope. He shoves them toward VINNIE.)* Here! Take these, roll 'em up an' sit on 'em!!

(VINNIE rushes to MARCO and grabs him, angrily.)

VINNIE. You listen to me, you little cockroach! Don't show off in front of your girlfriend. Don't you ever speak to me in that tone of voice. Even if maybe I did something wrong, you don't speak to your brother that way. I've known you since you were three hours old and I've been looking after you ever since!!

MARCO. That's the trouble, Vinnie—in your eyes I will always be three hours old ... seven pounds, eight ounces! Well, you don't have to look after me no more because I don't want to see you again as long as I live. *(VINNIE is taken aback by this statement. BETTY crosses to VINNIE.)*

BETTY. *(casually)* Vinnie, would you get me some ice cream?

VINNIE. Ice cream??! You want ice cream now??!

BETTY. No, of course not. I just want to talk to Marco, so please go to Kaufman's and get a pint of vanilla ice cream.

VINNIE. What do you want to do—make things worse?

BETTY. Could they be worse? Please.

VINNIE. *(after a thoughtful look at BETTY, crosses to the door)* Vanilla? *(He opens the door.)*

MARCO. Pay for the ice cream, Vin. Don't put the money in trust.

(VINNIE starts toward MARCO. BETTY stops him.)

BETTY. Vanilla. *(VINNIE exits. BETTY stands watching MARCO as he goes to the storeroom and brings out the drop cloth, paint and brush. He avoids looking at BETTY.)* What are you doing?

MARCO. I'm gonna finish the trim. Okay with you?

BETTY. If you want me to go for ice cream, too, just say so.

MARCO. Suit yourself. *(He starts painting the trim at the base of the wall.)*

BETTY. It would suit me to talk. You're mad at the world and I understand.

MARCO. *(turns to her, sharply)* You weren't comin' back, were ya? When you left here to go to Marilyn's, you weren't just sayin' ciao or adios. You was sayin' good-bye an' good luck. Lemme ask ya somethin'—you still in love with Henry Ritter?

BETTY. I was never in love with Henry Ritter.

MARCO. All I know is everything was whipped cream between you an' me until he showed up.

BETTY. Something he said upset me. He said I might hurt you some day.

MARCO. Vinnie said the same thing. Who'da dreamed that Vinnie Fabrizio an' Henry Ritter the third would see eye to eye? So, ya left like to protect me? Very nice o' you. Why'd ya come back? Just to tell me 'bout Vinnie? To pick up your food? Wash some dishes?

BETTY. I came back because my customary way of dealing with problems is running away from them. I don't want to do that anymore.

MARCO. No? So, how ya gonna deal with this problem?

BETTY. I'm not sure I know what my problem is.

MARCO. Really? Well, I can fill you in there. You see, you like me. Ya like me a lot, but you're not sure whether you like me for myself or because you hate your family. That's your problem, lady. Ya don't like Henry Ritter 'cause he's too close to home—too much like the family. That's where I come in. Ya walk in here with your frozen food an' what do ya find? A Dago kid with no education, never read "Little Women", don't know how to speak right, crude, no polish. Hotcha! That's for me. This'll knock the family right on their ass! Well, lemme tell ya somethin'—that don't make me feel like a million bucks! Ya know what you remind me of?

BETTY. Yes. You've made that perfectly clear.

MARCO. You remind me of The Statue O' Liberty. You

should stand out there in the harbor with a light an' ya could have printed on a T-shirt, "Gimme your weary an' your broke". What I mean, Betty, is you could do a lot better than *me*. You could hook up with some immigrant from Yugoslavia or maybe Korea who don't speak no English at all an' don't know nothin'. You could find a bigger loser than me. Ya wanna shaft the family? Hell, do it right!!

BETTY. Reminding you of The Statue Of Liberty isn't so bad. I thought you were going to say Lizzie Borden.

MARCO. I don't know her.

BETTY. Listen, Marco, don't tell me what I saw when I came in here because you don't know what you're talking about. I saw a very decent, law-abiding, compassionate fellow without much education, but with a very good mind. I saw a guy with a lot of potenial once he got out from under the influence of his brother.

MARCO. Do me a favor—leave Vinnie out o' this. He is a liar and a thief.

BETTY. Not really.

MARCO. Yeah, *really!* He talked me in to selling my half here for peanuts while he was selling out for a bundle an' then he tells me he's putting my share in trust.

BETTY. He meant it.

MARCO. He shoulda discussed it with me. He thinks o' me like I'm a child.

BETTY. Worse—*his* child. You're the son he'll never have. He doesn't know that he's kept you crippled all your life—calling you "kid"—giving you an idiot camera. You know, there's an old Italian saying. Never make your child better than you are. And it's as much your fault as his. You put him on a pedestal. You worshiped him.

MARCO. Well, he blew all that today! What really gets me is that not once did he say he was sorry—that he made a mistake. He did wrong.

BETTY. Nevertheless, it's the best thing he's ever done for you ... and he did admit he did something wrong.

MARCO. He said "*Maybe* I did something wrong"—like he's not sure.

BETTY. That's the most you're ever going to get out of Vinnie.

MARCO. It ain't enough.

BETTY. I promise you he knows he did wrong. He knows. And I don't think you should forget all the good things he did for you. He loves you—and you still love him in spite of this.

MARCO. What do ya expect me to do—forgive an' forget?! Never! No way!!

BETTY. Marco, I can not tell you how much I admire you. Truly, you are one of the most remarkable people I know. Obviously, you have never done one thing in your life that you are ashamed of—therefore, you never have to forgive anyone for anything. My God, how I envy you!!

(MARCO stares at her, thoughtfully, and slightly shaken. VINNIE enters carrying a paper bag with ice cream. He stands near the door looking at MARCO, uncertainly. MARCO turns and stares at VINNIE for a moment. MARCO crosses to VINNIE. They look at each other for a moment. MARCO smiles.)

MARCO. So? What'd ya bring me?

(VINNIE smiles and pulls MARCO into his arms.)

VINNIE. I knew you'd finally come to your senses.

(MARCO breaks away from VINNIE and is about to explode, but decides not to.)

MARCO. You could say that, Vin. I finally came to my senses. Now, let bygones be bygones an' when ya get the money from Addison, kindly hand me a check for my full share. Agreed?
VINNIE. *(Looks at MARCO for a moment, then nods.)* You got it.
MARCO. Okay, that's settled. *(He takes the bag from VINNIE and goes behind the counter. To Betty.)* Your ice cream is here. Want some?
BETTY. No.
MARCO. It's yours. He bought it for you. *(He drops the ice cream into the freezer, then takes the pad from the shelf and writes on it.)* One pint o' vanilla ice cream.
VINNIE. Marco, you know that little Greek restaurant on 82nd near Third?
MARCO. Christo's? Yeah—that's your friend.
VINNIE. He's looking to sell. It could be fixed up nice. Interested?
BETTY. I know Christo's. It's near the museum.
MARCO. I like that location. I'm interested.
VINNIE. Okay, I'll take you by there during the week and I'll make a deal for you.
MARCO. I know how to make a deal, Vinnie.
VINNIE. Yeah ... sure. Well, I've got some ideas for

you... if you want to hear them.

MARCO. Of course.

VINNIE. *(pleased)* Okay, we'll talk about it tomorrow night. It's Monday, so you'll be coming for dinner as usual.

MARCO. No.

VINNIE. What do you mean "no"?

MARCO. I hate that word "as usual." I am not doin' anything anymore *as usual.* I don't wanna be taken for granted. I am only comin' to your house for dinner when I am invited.

VINNIE. All right, you're invited.

MARCO. No. I want a proper invitation from the hostess—your wife, Fran.

VINNIE. Are you serious?

MARCO. Yeah, I'm serious. I'm not comin' every Monday like clockwork.

VINNIE. Well, now I don't know if there's time for Fran to get to the engraver by tomorrow night.

MARCO. The phone's okay. *(VINNIE glances at MARCO, walks quickly to the phone, deposits a coin and dials.)*

VINNIE. *(into phone)* Fran? I'm here with Marco. He wants to be invited to dinner tomorrow night . . . . Fran, I will explain later . . . . just shut up and do as I tell you. I have had one goddamn hell of a day.!! *(He holds the receiver out toward MARCO.)*

MARCO. (saunters to the phone and takes it from VIN-NIE) Hi, Fran, ... Dinner tomorrow night? Gee, Fran, I'm afraid I got this previous engagement with that friend I told ya 'bout, Miss Neal . . . . That's very nice o' you, but I gotta ask *her.* *(to BETTY)* My sister -in-law is inviting us to dinner tomorrow night. She's a good cook. What d'ya say?

BETTY. Sure! Tell her I'm coming even if you don't.

MARCO. *(into phone)* Fran? Thank you very much ... Uh... *(affectedly)* We'd be delighted!

CURTAIN

THE END

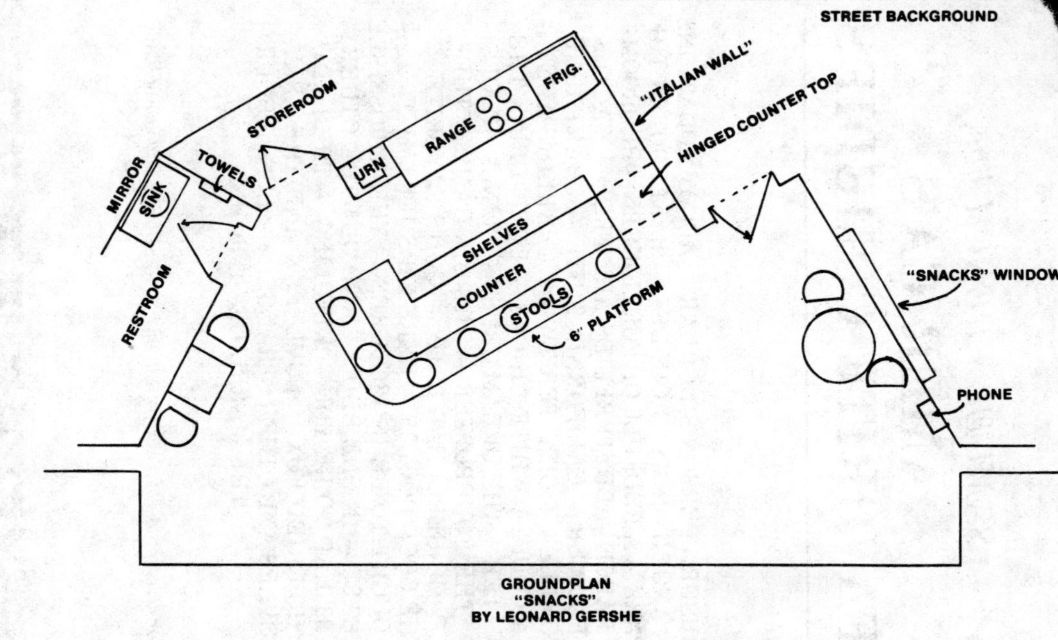

GROUNDPLAN
"SNACKS"
BY LEONARD GERSHE